This Journal is dedicated to...

To every girl who's learning to pray through her worries, glow through her challenges, and grow through her faith, this book is for you.

May these pages remind you that you are never too young, too unsure, or too imperfect for God to use you in amazing ways.

To the daughters, sisters, dreamers, and believers, keep shining, keep trusting, and keep growing.

Your glow is your testimony.

This journal belongs to:

____

ISBN: <u>978-1-972454-17-6</u>
Prayed Up, Glowed Up, and Growing
Copyright © 2025 by Yolanda Lance, B.A., M.Ed, Ed.S. with
Jah'Nay and Jae'Dyn McDowell

Yolanda Lance, Jah'Nay McDowell or Jae'Dyn McDowell
Conyers, GA
www.yolandipity.net
yolandipity@gmail.com or yolandaeducates@yahoo.com

All scriptures used are referenced from the King James Version of the Bible.
Printed in the United States of America

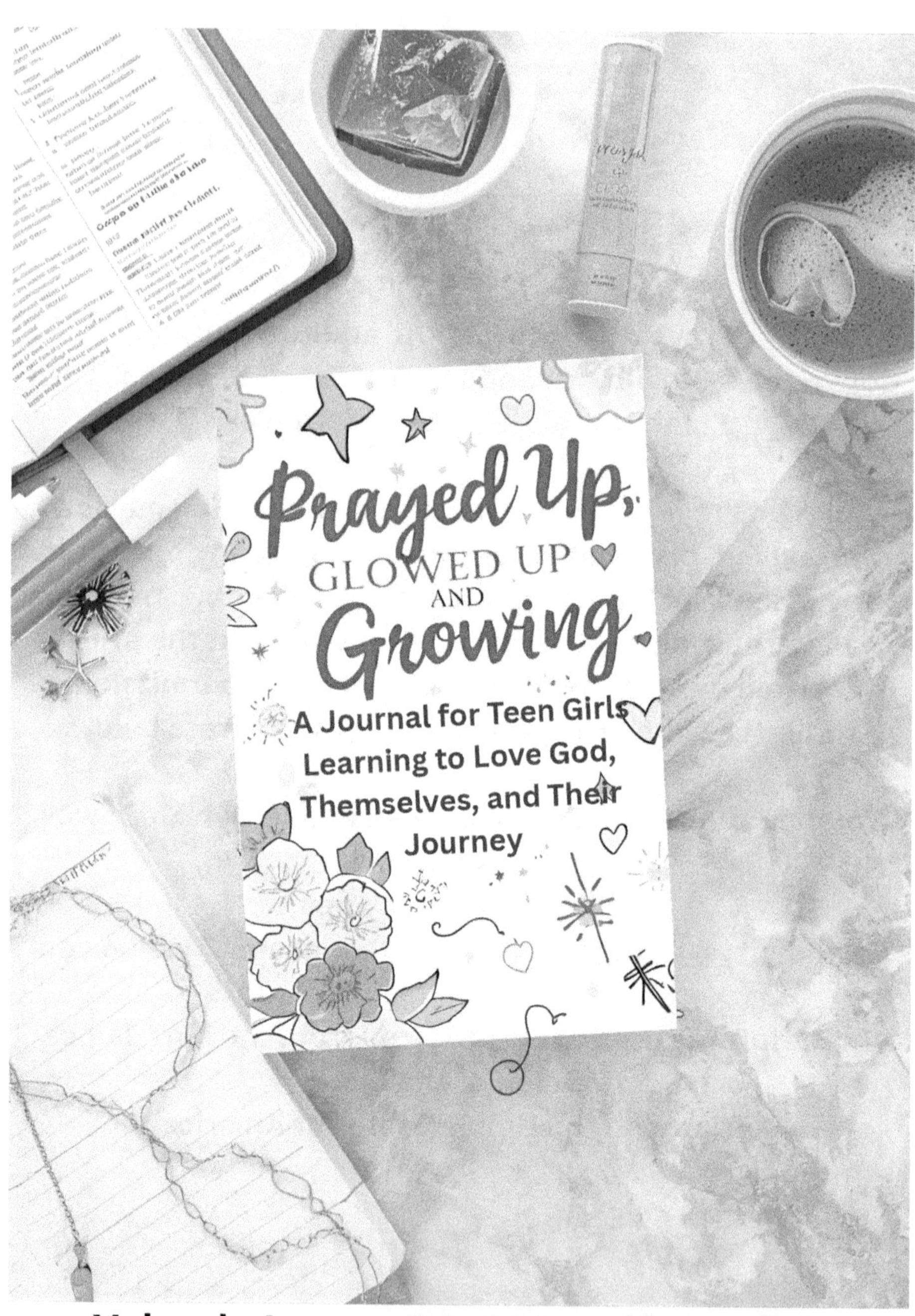

Yolanda Lance, BA, M.ED, ED.S., with Jah'Nay and Jae'Dyn McDowell

About the author

Yolanda Lance has spent over 20 years teaching middle school Language Arts and Reading, helping students discover the power of words and their own voices. Before becoming a teacher, she worked as a social worker, which deepened her heart for helping others. She and her daughters are co-owners of yolandipity.net.

She loves writing books that inspire women, children, and teens to grow in faith, confidence, and character. Every story or devotional she writes is filled with encouragement, biblical truth, and a reminder that God has a special plan for everyone.

Writing is a family passion! Along with her two daughters, Jah'Nay andJae'Dyn, who are her co-authors and editors, they have written and self-published over fourteen books. Together, they love traveling, exploring new adventures, and spending time with their adorable Frenchie, Koda, who never wants to miss a road trip!

We pray that you not only enjoy this journal, but that you find it to be beneficial to your growth in Christ.

The Snack-Sized Chapter Guide

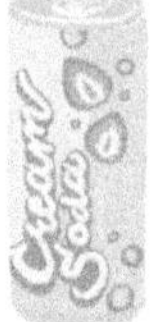

What It Does Means to Pray, Glow, and Grow???

To Pray:

Praying isn't about using fancy words or sounding perfect, it's just talking to God like you would talk to your best friend. When you pray, you're opening your heart, sharing your thoughts, and letting God know what's up. It's your way of saying, "Hey God, I trust You." Prayer keeps your heart calm, your faith strong, and your focus right where it needs to be, on Him.

Think of prayer as texting God... but with no typing limit and guaranteed delivery.

To Glow:

Your glow isn't about makeup, likes, or filters, it's what shines from inside. When you're walking with God, there's a light that people notice, peace, kindness, confidence, and joy. That's your God glow! It shows up when you smile through stress, forgive when it's hard, and love yourself the way God loves you. Your glow is proof that God's light lives in you.

To Grow:

Growing means learning, stretching, and trusting God even when it's uncomfortable. It's when you take what you pray about and actually start living it out. Growth happens when you make mistakes, learn lessons, and come back stronger, with God guiding every step. You don't have to be perfect to grow, you just have to keep going.

So remember...

When you pray, you **connect**. When you glow, you **reflect**. When you grow, you **become** everything God created you to be.
That's what Prayed Up, Glowed Up, and Growing is all about, a journey of talking to God, shining His light, and becoming your best self through Him.

# 1. Knowing Your Worth

God didn't make you to be a remix, He made you the original track. Stop comparing your behind-the-scenes to someone else's highlight reel. You are valuable, loved, and wonderfully made just as you are. Let's be real, the world will try to tell you who you are every single day. It'll say you need to look a certain way, act a certain way, or have a certain number of likes to matter. But here's the real truth: you already have worth, real, God-given worth, and **nobody** can take that away.

Your worth isn't found in your grades, your clothes, or who texts you back. It's found in Who made you. You were created on purpose, for a purpose. (Psalm 139:14 says you are "fearfully and wonderfully made.")

When you know your worth, you'll stop settling for less, less respect, less love, and less peace. You will start walking with your head high because you know God doesn't make mistakes. You will learn to say, "I'm not perfect, but I'm valuable."

Knowing your worth helps you make better choices, protect your heart, and treat others (and yourself!) with kindness. Because when you see yourself the way God sees you, girl... that's when you will truly glow.

Scripture

Psalm 139:14 – "I praise You because I am fearfully and wonderfully made."

Reflective Questions:

What makes me special in God's eyes?

____

____

How do I act when I truly believe I'm worthy?

____

____

Who reminds me of my worth when I forget?

____

____

What lie about my worth do I need to stop believing?

____

____

How can I remind another girl that she's valuable too?

____

____

Faith Challenge:

Write one affirmation about yourself and tape it on your mirror. Read it every day this week.

Riddle:

I'm not found in mirrors or things you buy,
Not in likes or looks that pass you by.
I'm placed within by the One above—
What am I, wrapped in endless love?

# 2. Faith Over Fear

Fear is loud, but faith is louder. The next time you're nervous about speaking up or trying something new, remember, God's already at the finish line cheering you on. Picture this, you're standing at the edge of a diving board, looking down at the water. Your knees are shaking, your heart's racing, and your brain's screaming, "Nope!" But then, you take a deep breath and jump anyway, that's what faith over fear feels like.

Having faith over fear doesn't mean you never get scared. It means you trust God even when you are. It's choosing to believe that God's got you, even when things look uncertain, uncomfortable, or totally out of control. Fear says, "What if I fail?" Faith says, "Even if I fall, God will help me get back up." Fear says, "I'm not enough."

Faith says, "God made me enough." Fear tries to shrink you. Faith reminds you that with God, you're unstoppable. (Check out 2 Timothy 1:7, "For God has not given us a spirit of fear, but of power, love, and a sound mind.") When you choose faith over fear, you stop letting your worries drive the car of your heart, mind, soul, and spirit. You let God take the wheel instead. That's how your courage starts to glow, even in the dark.

Reflective Questions:

What's something that scares me right now?

____

____

How has God helped me overcome fear before?

____

____

What verse or prayer helps calm me when I'm afraid?

____

____

Who can I talk to when I need courage?

____

____

What would I do if I wasn't afraid to fail?

____

____

What fear do I want to face with God's help?

____

____

How can prayer make me braver?

____

____

Faith Challenge:
Pray for courage before doing something that scares you.

Riddle:
Why did the scared Bible verse hide under the bed?

3. Purpose and Calling

You don't need to have your whole life figured out by 16. God's GPS reroutes better than Google Maps. Just keep moving in faith, even if you're only sure of your next step.

Think of **purpose** as the reason God made you, like your personal mission in life, and **calling** as how He wants you to use it.

Maybe your purpose is to help people, create art, make others laugh, or change the world one kind act at a time.

Your calling is how you live that out! So don't stress if you don't have it all figured out yet, God's basically your GPS, and even when you take the wrong turn, He'll still reroute you to where you're meant to be.

Scripture:

Jeremiah 29:11 "For I know the plans I have for you," declares the Lord.

Reflective Questions:

What are my biggest dreams or goals?

____

____

What comes naturally to me that could be part of my purpose?

____

____

What's one small step I could make toward my purpose? _______________________________

____

How can I use my gifts to serve others?

____

____

What makes me feel most connected to God's plan for my life? _________________________

____

____

How can I trust His timing when I can't see the full picture?

____

____

Faith Challenge:

Write down one dream God has placed in your heart for your life and pray over it every morning.

____

____

Riddle:

Why did the pencil pray before writing?

4. Self-Love & Acceptance

Self-love doesn't mean loving your selfies, it means loving your soul. God made you with intention, from your curls to your quirks. Be kind to the girl in the mirror, she's a masterpiece in progress. Let's get one thing straight, loving yourself isn't being selfish. It's understanding that you are God's creation, and He didn't make a single mistake when He made you.

Self-love is about being kind to yourself, even on the days when you feel awkward, unsure, or not "enough." It's giving yourself the same grace you'd give your best friend. It's saying, "Yeah, I have flaws, but I'm still amazing because God says so."

Acceptance means stopping the habit of comparing yourself to everyone else. You don't have to look like her, sound like her, or live like her, because your path is different.

Psalm 139:14 says, "I praise You because I am fearfully and wonderfully made." That means every inch of you, inside and out, was designed with purpose. When you learn to love and accept yourself, you stop trying to earn approval from people who didn't create you. You start walking confidently, knowing that your value doesn't change based on opinions, it comes from God, who calls you His masterpiece (Ephesians 2:10).

So, look in the mirror and smile, not because you're perfect, but because you're perfectly loved.

Reflective Questions:
What do I love about who I am right now?

____

____

What's one way I can show myself kindness today?

____

____

How does God see me, even when I feel insecure?

____

____

What negative thought about myself needs to be replaced with truth?

____

____

How can I help another girl feel confident about who she is?

____

____

How can I show myself grace today?

____

____

Faith Challenge:
Write a love note to yourself from God's perspective.

____

____

____

Riddle:
Why did the mirror start singing gospel music?

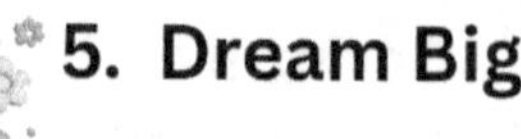 # 5. Dream Big

Young lady, God didn't give you small dreams, He gave you big ones that stretch your faith, challenge your fears, and make you grow. Dreaming big isn't about chasing fame or fancy stuff; it's about believing that God can do something amazing through you.

Sometimes people will say, "That's impossible," or "You're thinking too big." But guess what? God specializes in impossible (Luke 1:37, "For with God, nothing will be impossible."). Your dreams aren't "too much" for God. He's the same God who made galaxies, your big ideas don't scare Him. So write them down, vision board it out, and let your faith work harder than your fear.

Dreaming big means seeing yourself the way God sees you, full of potential, purpose, and power. It's about trusting that even small beginnings can lead to great things when you keep walking in faith. Don't shrink your dreams to fit your comfort zone or anyone else's. Expand your faith to match God's plans. Pray about your dreams, work hard, and stay humble, because when God is part of your vision, it's not just a dream... it's a destiny!

Remember, your dream isn't too crazy, too late, or too much, it's just waiting for your faith to catch up.

Scripture
Matthew 19:26, "With God, all things are possible."

Reflective Questions:

What's a big dream I have that excites me?

____

____

How can I use that dream to honor God?

____

____

What step can I take toward it this week?

____

____

Who inspires me to chase my dreams faithfully?

____

____

What fears have been holding me back from dreaming bigger?

____

____

Faith Challenge:
Create a mini vision board with your top three goals.

Riddle:
Why did the dream take a nap?

Here are two fun and creative ways to make vision boards, along with easy step-by-step directions for each!

1. Classic Poster Board Vision Board

Perfect for: hands-on, crafty girls who love cutting and gluing!

You'll need: Poster board or corkboard, Magazines, printed pictures, or photos, Scissors and glue/tape, Markers, stickers, washi tape (optional)

Directions: Set your goals. Think about what you want in the next year, school, friendships, hobbies, confidence, travel, etc. Find your visuals. Cut out words and pictures that represent your dreams and feelings. Arrange before gluing. Play around with the layout until it feels inspiring and balanced. Glue and decorate. Add doodles, quotes, or stickers for personality.

Display it. Hang it somewhere you'll see every day, like your bedroom wall or closet door.

2. Digital Vision Board (Canva or Pinterest)

Perfect for: tech-loving teens or those who prefer a neat, modern look.

You'll need: A free Canva account or a Pinterest board, A phone, tablet, or computer.

Directions (Canva version): Open Canva → search for "Vision Board Template." Upload images or use free ones from Canva that match your goals and dreams. Add text and affirmations. Include words like "Confidence," "Adventure," "Peace," etc. Save your design. Set it as your phone wallpaper or print it out.

Directions (Pinterest version): Create a new board and title it "My Vision Board." Pin photos and quotes that represent your goals and dreams.

Visit your board often, add new pins as your goals evolve!

Teen Tip #1

Know Who You Are in Christ. You are God's masterpiece, created with love, purpose, and strength. Your value comes from who you are in Christ, not what others think. So when you look in the mirror, say, "I'm God's Masterpiece."

 # 6. Dealing with Racism

Let's be real, racism hurts. It's unfair, it's ugly, and it's something no one should ever have to experience. But even when people treat you unfairly because of the color of your skin, remember this: your worth doesn't change. God made you exactly how He wanted you, skin tone, hair texture, culture, and all , and He called it "good." (Genesis 1:31).

Dealing with racism takes strength, but it also takes faith. You don't have to fight hate with hate, you can fight it with wisdom, courage, and love that comes from God. That doesn't mean staying silent. It means standing strong, speaking truth with grace, and remembering that your identity is rooted in who God says you are, not in what the world says about you.

It's hard when people judge you before they know you. But remember, you're not called to be bitter, you're called to be better. Keep your crown straight and your heart right; love is stronger than hate every time.

When you face racism, talk to someone you trust, pray about it, and remember Jesus understands what it feels like to be mistreated. He turned pain into purpose, and you can, too.

Romans 12:21 says, "Do not be overcome by evil, but overcome evil with good."

So, walk tall, speak truth, and shine bright. Your light, your culture, your voice, they matter more than you know.

Reflective Questions:

How have I experienced unfair treatment?

____

____

How can I respond with strength and grace instead of anger? _______________________________________

____

Who encourages me to stay strong? ________________

____

How can I help others facing similar struggles?

____

____

How does God's love remind me of my value?

____

____

Who helps me feel proud of who I am?

____

____

Faith Challenge:

Pray for someone who hurt you and ask God to give you strength to forgive.

Riddle:

Why did love win the race?

# 7. Friendship & Loyalty

Good friends are like sunshine, they make life brighter, warmer, and way more fun. But true friendship isn't just about selfies, sleepovers, or matching bracelets. It's about showing up, staying real, and keeping promises, even when things aren't easy.

Loyalty means being there for your friends, not just when life's good, but when it's messy, too. It's choosing to be honest, kind, and supportive even when gossip or drama tries to pull you in. Proverbs 17:17 says, "A friend loves at all times." That means real friendship doesn't fade when you disagree or when someone else comes along. It's about loving people the way Jesus loves us, with grace, patience, and forgiveness.

Here's the truth: You don't need a ton of friends, you just need a few who pray with you, cheer for you, and tell you the truth (even when you don't want to hear it). And don't forget, being a good friend means being that kind of person yourself. So, keep your circle full of love, not drama. The right friends don't just hang out, they help you grow and glow. The reality is, true friends are like Wi-Fi, you don't always see them working, but you know when they're gone. Keep friends who pray for you, not just post with you.

Reflective Questions:

Who are my closest friends and why?

____

____

How do I show loyalty to my friends?

____

____

What qualities do I look for in a friend?

____

____

How do I handle disagreements with friends?

____

____

How can I be a blessing to my friends this week?

____

____

Faith Challenge:
Reach out to a friend and say something encouraging from
God's Word.

Riddle:
Why did the best friend bring glue to church?

 # 8. Social Media Pressure

Okay, let's be honest, social media can be a lot. One minute you're just scrolling for funny videos, and the next you're comparing your life to someone who looks like they've got it all together. **But here's the truth:** what you see online is not the whole story.

Everyone posts their highlight reel, the smiles, the vacations, the perfect selfies, but not the bad days, breakouts, or tears. It's easy to feel like you're not enough, but remember this: you were already enough before the filters.

Social media pressure tricks you into thinking your value comes from likes, followers, or comments. Likes fade, God's love doesn't. Don't let filters fool you, real life happens off-screen. You're more than your follower count; you're fully loved, right where you are. But your worth isn't measured by an app, it's defined by God, who already calls you chosen, loved, and valuable. (1 Peter 2:9)

It's okay to unplug sometimes. Real life, the people who love you, the moments that make you laugh, the goals you're chasing, that's where true joy lives. When you spend more time with God than your news feed, you start to glow for real. So post what's real, not what's perfect. Be the light, not the algorithm. And remember: your glow doesn't need a filter.

Scripture: Colossians 3:2
"Set your minds on things above, not on earthly things."

Reflective Questions:

How does social media affect how I see myself?

____

____

When do I feel pressured online?

____

____

How can I focus more on God than comparison?

____

____

How can I use social media to encourage others?

____

____

What boundaries can I set for my social media use?

____

____

What would it look like to use social media for good?

____

____

Faith Challenge:
Post something encouraging or uplifting online this week.

Riddle:
Why did the phone pray before posting?

# 9. Staying Positive in Hard Times

Let's be real, life isn't always sunshine and selfies. Sometimes things just hurt. Maybe a friend turns on you, your grades slip, or you're dealing with something way heavier than anyone realizes. In those moments, staying positive can feel impossible.

But here's the secret: positivity doesn't mean pretending everything's fine. It means choosing to believe that God is still working, even when life feels broken. It's about holding onto hope, even if it's just a tiny piece. When life feels heavy, joy is your secret weapon.

When you stay positive, you're not ignoring your problems, you're simply remembering that your problems don't get the last word. God does. Romans 8:28 says, "And we know that in all things God works for the good of those who love Him." Sometimes positivity looks like crying, praying, and saying, "God, I don't get it, but I trust You." Other times, it's putting on your favorite song, laughing with your friends, playing with your siblings, and reminding yourself that a tough season won't last forever.

So when life gets heavy, lift your chin, fix your eyes on God, and keep your glow shining. Storms may shake you, but they can't stop your light.

Scripture:
Nehemiah 8:10, "The joy of the Lord is my strength."

Reflective Questions:

What brings me joy and helps me stay hopeful, even on hard days?

____

____

How can I focus on God when things are tough?

____

____

Who encourages me when I'm down?

____

____

How can I share my joy with others?

____

____

What positive habits help me stay hopeful?

____

____

How can I find joy in small things?

____

____

Faith Challenge: Write down three blessings you notice each day this week.

Riddle: Why did the smile bring an umbrella?

# 10. Self-Care & Healthy Habits

Self-care isn't selfish, girl, it's necessary. God wants you to take care of the body, mind, and heart He gave you. Think of self-care as giving yourself the same love, attention, and kindness you'd give your best friend.

Healthy habits aren't just about eating your veggies (though that helps 😉). They're about creating routines that keep your body strong, your mind clear, and your spirit connected to God.

That means: eating nutritious food and drinking water, getting enough sleep and rest, exercising in ways that make you feel alive, taking time to pray, journaling, or just sitting in God's presence, and setting boundaries with people or situations that drain you.

1 Corinthians 6:19-20 reminds us that our bodies are temples of the Holy Spirit. Treating yourself well isn't optional, it's honoring God. Self-care also includes your feelings. If you're stressed, sad, or overwhelmed, don't ignore it. Talk to God, pray it out, and ask for guidance. Your glow shines brightest when your heart and body are cared for.

Remember: Healthy habits today make it easier to shine, grow, and walk confidently in God's plan for tomorrow.

Reflective Questions:

How do I currently care for my body? _______________

____

What healthy habits can I start this week?

____

____

How does self-care help me focus on God?

____

____

When do I feel my best physically and mentally?

____

____

How can I encourage someone else to practice self-care?

____

____

Faith Challenge:

Pick one new healthy habit to try this week. OR try one of these:

Hydration Nation! 💧 Because your body is 70% water, not 70% iced coffee. Drink up before you dry up!

Sleep Like a Queen. 👑 Beauty sleep isn't a myth — it's a miracle. Eight hours = less drama, more glow.

Snack Smart (Most of the Time). 🍓🍞 Fruit is great, but fries are feelings. Balance, girl, balance.

Move That Miracle Body. 🕺🎶 Dance like no one's watching (except your dog), stretch, walk, or pretend you're in a music video. It counts!

Talk Nice to Yourself. 💬💚 You wouldn't let anyone trash, talk your bestie, so don't do it to yourself, you're God's masterpiece.

Riddle:

Why did the water bottle go to church?

11. "Forgiving Others" and Letting Go

Scripture: "Be kind and compassionate to one another, forgiving each other." – Ephesians 4:32

Forgiving Others & Letting Go!

Forgiving people isn't saying, "What you did was okay," it's saying, "I'm not carrying that mess around in your heart and anymore." When you hold onto anger, it's like drinking sour milk and hoping the other person gets a stomachache.

Let it go!,

Let God handle it, and free up your heart for better things, like peace, joy, maybe some salty and crispy French fries.

Holding grudges is like keeping old text messages from people you don't even talk to anymore, pointless and taking up space! God wants you to let that stuff go so your heart has room for peace and joy. And again, when you forgive, you're not saying they were right, you're just saying, "I'm too blessed to be this stressed." So hit that mental delete button and move on with your glow! Your peace is worth more than your pride.

Reflective Questions:

Who or what do I need to let go of today?

____

____

How does forgiving free me too?

____

____

What "old messages" or memories might you still be holding
onto that are taking up space in your heart?

____

____

How does forgiving someone free you more than it frees the
other person?

____

____

What's one practical way you can "hit delete" on hurt this
week and make room for peace and joy?

____

____

Faith Challenge:
Say a quick prayer for the person who hurt you. I know, it's
tough, but that's next-level faith right there.

Riddle:
Why did the grudge get kicked off the bus?

Teen Tip #2

Guard Your Heart and Mind. Protect your peace. Fill your thoughts with things that are true, kind, and uplifting.

Guard Your Heart and Mind

Guard your heart, it's precious gold,
A treasure chest no thief should hold.
Keep your peace — let worries fade,
God's calm will cover what He made.
Let truth be roots that keep you strong,
Let kindness fill your every song.
Think on the good, the pure, the bright,
And fill your soul with Heaven's light.
When storms arise or doubts appear,
Remember, God's still always near.
Protect your joy, your sacred space —
Let His love guard your heart in grace.

12. Body Confidence

Let's be real, it's easy to feel insecure about your body. Between social media, magazines, and even friends' comments, it can feel like you're never "good enough." But here's the truth: your body is amazing because God made it amazing.

Body confidence isn't about looking perfect or fitting into a certain size. It's about loving yourself as you are and trusting that God created you on purpose. Psalm 139:14 says, "I praise You because I am fearfully and wonderfully made." That means every curve, freckle, and curl is intentional. Confidence comes when you treat your body with respect: move it in ways that make you feel strong and happy, fuel it with nourishing foods, rest when it needs rest, and speak kindly to yourself instead of being critical. You might not love every single thing about your reflection, but guess what? God does! Stand proud, move with confidence, and remember: He designed you with care.

Remember: when you honor your body, you're honoring God. You don't need someone else's approval, your worth doesn't change with a number on a scale or a like on a post. Glow with confidence because your Creator made you exactly as you're supposed to be.

Scripture:

1 Corinthians 6:19 – "Your body is a temple of the Holy Spirit."

Reflective Questions:

What part of my body do I feel grateful for today?

____

____

How can I celebrate and take care of my body this week?

____

____

What negative thoughts about my appearance do I need to replace?

____

____

Who encourages me to feel confident?

____

____

How can I inspire body positivity in my friends?

____

____

Faith Challenge:

Stand in front of the mirror and say **three** positive things about yourself out loud.

1. ____

2. ____

3. ____

Riddle:

Why did the mirror smile back?

13. Prayer Life

Prayer isn't just a checklist or something you do at bedtime, it's your personal conversation with God. Think of it like texting your BFF, but better: He always reads your messages, never leaves you on "read," and gives advice you can actually trust. Building a strong prayer life means talking to God about everything, the good, the bad, the funny, and the confusing. It's also about listening, paying attention to how He might be guiding you. Some days you'll pray a lot, some days it's just a quick "God, help me today," and that's totally okay. Prayer doesn't need fancy words or long speeches. Talk to God about everything, your fears, dreams, or even what happened at lunch. He listens.

Why have a prayer life? **Because it:**
helps you stay grounded when life gets messy, strengthens your trust in God, gives you peace in scary or uncertain moments, and lets you celebrate your wins and ask for guidance in challenges.

Philippians 4:6-7 says, "Do not be anxious about anything, but in every situation, by prayer and petition, with thanksgiving, present your requests to God. And the peace of God... will guard your hearts and your minds in Christ Jesus."

Your prayer life is like a glow-up for your soul, the more you do it, the brighter your faith shines.

Scripture: 1 Thessalonians 5:17 – "Pray without ceasing."

Please understand, God listens to voice notes straight from your heart, even if you're whispering, crying, or laughing mid-prayer.

Reflective Questions:

What do I talk to God about most?

____

____

How can I make prayer part of my daily routine?

____

____

When do I feel closest to God?

____

____

What prayers have God answered recently?

____

____

How can I encourage a friend to pray?

____

____

Faith Challenge:
Write a short prayer each morning this week.

Riddle: Why did the phone go to church?

Dear God, ____

____

____

____

____

Dear God, ____

____

____

____

____

Dear God, ____

____

____

____

____

Dear God, ____

____

____

____

____

Dear God, ____

____

____

____

____

Prayer Prompts

Dear God, _______________________________________

____
____
____

Dear God, _______________________________________

____
____
____

Dear God, _______________________________________

____
____
____

Dear God, _______________________________________

____
____
____

Dear God, _______________________________________

____
____
____

 # 14. Confidence in Christ

Confidence in Christ isn't about being the loudest, the most popular, or having everything figured out. It's about knowing who you are in God and trusting that He has a plan for your life.
When you're confident in Christ, you don't let other people's opinions or mistakes define you.

When you are confident in Christ, you understand that you are:

Loved — nothing can separate you from God's love (Romans 8:38-39)
Chosen — He made you for a purpose (Ephesians 2:10)
Strong — He equips you to face challenges (Philippians 4:13)

Confidence in Christ comes from prayer, reading His Word, and remembering that your identity isn't based on likes, grades, or achievements, it's based on what God says about you.
When you walk in His confidence, fear and doubt shrink. You shine brighter because your value and strength come from Him, not from the world.
Remember: Your confidence doesn't come from being perfect, it comes from being His. When you rely on God, even your shadow shines brighter.

Scripture:
Proverbs 3:26 – "The Lord will be your confidence."

Reflective Questions:

What makes me feel confident in God's strength?

____

____

How can I trust God when I feel insecure?

____

____

Who inspires me to be courageous?

____

____

How can I remind myself of God's promises?

____

____

How can I show confidence in faith to others?

____

____

How can I walk boldly this week?

____

____

Faith Challenge:
Recite one Bible verse aloud to boost your confidence each day.

Riddle:
Why did the lightbulb glow so brightly?

15. Making Wise Choices

Life is full of choices, big ones, small ones, and everything in between. Some are obvious, like choosing homework over video games, or choosing pizza over salad. Others are trickier, like choosing friends, how you speak to someone, or how you spend your time online.

Making wise choices doesn't mean being perfect, it means thinking, praying, and trusting God before you act. When you rely on God's guidance, your decisions reflect His wisdom instead of just what's easy, popular, or fun.

Proverbs 3:5-6 says, "Trust in the Lord with all your heart and lean not on your own understanding; in all your ways submit to Him, and He will make your paths straight."

Wise choices can:

- Keep you safe physically, emotionally, and spiritually
- Protect your heart and relationships
- Help you grow into the person God created you to be

Remember, sometimes mistakes happen, and that's okay. The key is learning from them, asking God for forgiveness if needed, and making a better choice next time. Your glow grows when your choices honor God and reflect His love.

Scripture: James 1:5 – "If any of you lacks wisdom, let him ask of God."

Reflective Questions:

What choice am I facing right now?

____

____

How can I seek God's guidance in decisions?

____

____

Who do I trust to give wise advice, when I am unsure?

____

____

When have I made a good choice after praying?

____

____

How can I encourage others to make wise decisions?

____

____

Faith Challenge:
Pray before making one decision this week.

Riddle:
Why did the brain go to Bible study?

 # 16. Family Love

Family isn't always perfect, sometimes it's messy, loud, or confusing. But family is one of the first ways God can show us love. Whether it's parents, siblings, cousins, or even close friends who feel like family, these relationships are meant to teach us patience, forgiveness, and unconditional love.

Family love means:

- Being there for each other, even when it's hard
- Supporting and encouraging one another
- Forgiving mistakes and letting go of grudges
- Celebrating wins together and comforting each other in losses

Ephesians 6:1-3 reminds us, "Children, obey your parents in the Lord, for this is right. Honor your father and mother," which comes with a promise of blessings.

Even when family drives you crazy, remember that God created each family to help you grow in love, faith, and character. When you choose kindness, patience, and understanding, your home can become a place where God's love shines through, and your glow spreads to everyone around you.

Scripture:
Exodus 20:12 – "Honor your father and your mother."

Family can be loud, funny, annoying, or all three, but they're yours. Loving them shows God's love through you.

Reflective Questions:
What's one thing I appreciate about my family?

____

____

How can I show love to my family today?

____

____

How do I handle conflicts at home?

____

____

Who in my family encourages me spiritually?

____

____

What family traditions or moments make me happy?

____

____

Faith Challenge:
Write a note of gratitude to a family member this week.

Riddle:
Why did the family sit at the dinner table?

Dear __________________________________
I love you and I appreciate and I am grateful
for...

____

____

____

____

____

____

____

____

____

____

____

____

____

____

____

Teen Tip #3

Choose Friends Who Lift You Up. True friends encourage you, celebrate your wins, and help you stay strong in faith.

# 17. Handling Anger

Anger is totally normal, we all feel it sometimes. Maybe someone hurt you, frustrated you, or things just didn't go your way. **But here's the key:** how you respond to anger matters more than feeling it.

Handling anger in a healthy way means:
- Taking a pause before reacting
- Praying or talking to God about what's bothering you
- Expressing your feelings without hurting yourself or others
- Choosing forgiveness instead of holding grudges.

Ephesians 4:26-27 says, "In your anger do not sin: Do not let the sun go down while you are still angry, and do not give the devil a foothold." That means it's okay to be upset, but don't let anger control your actions.

Controlled anger can actually protect you and set boundaries, but uncontrolled anger can damage friendships, family relationships, and your peace of mind. When you let God guide your emotions, you turn a potentially messy moment into a chance to grow, shine, and show self-control. Anger is like hot sauce, okay in small doses, but dangerous if you pour too much. Feel it, but don't let it control you.

Scripture:
"Be angry and do not sin." – Ephesians 4:26

Reflective Questions:

What triggers my anger most of the time?

____

____

What can I do to calm down before reacting?

____

____

Who helps me when I'm upset?

____

____

How can I express my feelings in a healthy way?

____

____

How does God help me handle anger?

____

____

Faith Challenge:
Pray or journal the next time you feel angry instead of
reacting immediately.

Riddle:
Why did the soda can pray for patience?

18. Dealing with Disappointment

Disappointment stinks, let's be real. Maybe a plan fell through, a friend let you down, or something you hoped for just didn't happen. It's normal to feel sad, frustrated, or even angry. But how you handle it can make a huge difference in your heart and your glow.

Dealing with disappointment means:
- Being honest with your feelings instead of hiding them
- Talking to God about how you feel (He gets it!)
- Looking for lessons or ways to grow from the situation
- Trusting that God has a bigger plan, even when you don't understand it

Romans 8:28 reminds us, "And we know that in all things God works for the good of those who love Him." Even when life doesn't go the way you want, God is still working behind the scenes. Disappointment doesn't define you, your response does. When you let God guide you through tough moments, you turn setbacks into opportunities to gain strength, wisdom, and hope.

Scripture:

Psalm 34:18 – "The Lord is close to the brokenhearted."

Reflective Questions:

What recent disappointment do I need to give to God?

____

____

How can I trust God's plan when things don't go as expected?

____

____

Who can I talk to for encouragement?

____

____

What can I learn from disappointment?

____

____

How has God surprised me before?

____

____

Faith Challenge:

Write a letter to God about a disappointment and thank Him for future blessings.

Dear God, _______________________________________

____

____

____

____

____

Riddle:

Why did the closed door smile?

19. Comparison

Let's be honest, it's super easy to compare yourself to others, especially on social media, at school, or even with friends. But here's the truth: comparison steals your joy and dims your glow. God made you unique, with your own gifts, personality, and purpose. No one else has your exact combination of talents, dreams, and experiences, and that's a good thing! Psalm 139:14 says, "I praise You because I am fearfully and wonderfully made."
Comparison can make you feel "less than," jealous, or insecure.

But when you focus on God's plan for your life, you start to:

- Appreciate your own strengths and journey
- Celebrate others without feeling threatened
- Grow in confidence and gratitude, instead of asking, "Why can't I be like her?" ask, "How can I use what God gave me to shine?"

When you stop comparing and start embracing your uniqueness, your light starts to shine brighter than ever. Scrolling can make you think everyone's life is perfect, but highlight reels aren't real life. Run your own race, not someone else's.

Scripture:
Galatians 6:4, "Each one should test their own actions."

Scrolling can make you think everyone's life is perfect, but highlight reels aren't real life. Run your own race, not someone else's.

Reflective Questions:
When do I compare myself to others most?

____

____

How does comparison affect my self-esteem?

____

____

What unique gifts has God given me?

____

____

How can I celebrate others without comparing myself?

____

____

What steps can I take to focus on my journey?

____

____

Faith Challenge:
Write down three things that make you unique.

1.____

2.____

3.____

Riddle:
Why did the turtle stop looking at the rabbit?

20. Gratitude

Gratitude isn't just about saying "thank you," it's about seeing life the way God wants you to see it. When you focus on what you have instead of what you don't, your heart feels lighter, your mood lifts, and your glow grows brighter.
Being grateful doesn't mean ignoring struggles or pretending life is perfect.

It means noticing the little blessings:

- A kind word from a friend
- A sunny day or a cozy hoodie
- Your talents, family, or even pizza nights

1 Thessalonians 5:18 says, "Give thanks in all circumstances; for this is God's will for you in Christ Jesus." Even in tough times, gratitude helps you trust that God is working for your good.

When you practice gratitude, you start to appreciate your own journey, celebrate others' wins without jealousy, and see life as full of possibilities. It's hard to be grumpy when you're busy counting your blessings, and that's a glow you can't fake!

Gratitude can turn "ugh" days into "okay" days and "okay" days into "amazing" ones. The more you thank God, the more joy sneaks in.

Reflective Questions:

What are three things I'm thankful for today?

____

____

How does gratitude change my mood?

____

____

How can I thank God more each day?

____

____

Who can I show gratitude to this week?

____

____

How does being thankful help me face challenges?

____

____

Faith Challenge:
Start a gratitude jar and write one thing you're thankful for each day.

Riddle:
Why did the thankful heart sing all day?

 **21. Staying Pure**

Staying pure isn't just about what you do with your body, it's about protecting your heart, your mind, and your spirit. It means making choices that honor God, yourself, and your future. Purity is about respect: for yourself, for others, and ultimately for God's plan for your life.

This is what staying pure looks like:
- Setting boundaries in friendships and relationships
- Thinking before you act or speak
- Choosing media, conversations, and environments that build you up
- Waiting on God's timing for big decisions

1 Thessalonians 4:3-4 says, "For this is the will of God, your sanctification: that you abstain from sexual immorality; that each of you know how to control your own body in holiness and honor." Purity isn't about being perfect, it's about being intentional and trusting God to guide your choices. When you stay true to your values, you glow with confidence, self-respect, and God's approval.

Scripture:
Matthew 5:8, "Blessed are the pure in heart."

Purity isn't about being perfect, it's about keeping your heart focused on God. Shine bright by staying true to your values, even when the world says "do whatever."

Reflective Questions:

What does purity mean to me?

____

____

How can I keep my heart focused on God?

____

____

What helps me make pure choices?

____

____

How do I respond when others pressure me?

____

____

How can I honor God in my relationships?

____

____

Faith Challenge:

Write a personal promise to honor God in one area of your life this week.

My personal promise: _______________________

____

____

Riddle:

Why did the heart wear sunglasses?

Teen Tip #4

Take Care of Your Body and Mind

Your body is a gift from God. Rest, eat well, move joyfully, and speak kindly to yourself.

A Gift from God

Your body's a temple, precious and true,
A gift from God, entrusted to you.
Rest when you're weary,
breathe and be still,
Let peace refill what the world tries to
steal.
Eat what gives strength, move with delight,
Dance in the sunlight,
sleep through the night.
Be gentle in thought, speak kindness inside,
Let grace be the mirror where love can
reside.
You're fearfully made, both body and soul,
Complete in His image, beautifully whole.
So care for this vessel, honor His art —
Keep joy in your spirit and love in your
heart.

22. Faith in the Future

Sometimes the future feels scary or uncertain, like, "What if I mess up?" or "What if things don't go my way?" That's normal! But having faith in the future means trusting that God is already there, working things out for your good.

Faith in the future looks like:

- Believing God has a plan, even if you can't see it yet
- Making choices today that honor Him
- Knowing He will guide your tomorrow
- Stay hopeful when things don't seem to make sense
- Praying about your dreams, worries, and goals
- Trusting God's timing

Jeremiah 29:11 says, "For I know the plans I have for you, declares the Lord, plans to prosper you and not to harm you, plans to give you hope and a future."
You're walking into His plan, not into the unknown. Faith in the future isn't just sitting around waiting, it's walking with God today, trusting Him for tomorrow. When you do that, your confidence grows, your heart stays light, and your glow gets brighter with every step.

The future can feel scary, but God already has your back. His plans are bigger than your worries. Step forward with courage, knowing He's paving the way.

Scripture: "Faith is confidence in what we hope for." – Hebrews 11:1
Scripture: Jeremiah 29:11, "For I know the plans I have for you," declares the Lord.

Reflective Questions:

What excites me about my future? _________________________
____
____

What worries me about what's ahead? _____________________
____
____

How can I trust God with my future plans? _________________
____
____

Who inspires me to have faith for tomorrow? _______________
____
____

What steps can I take now to prepare for God's plan?
____
____

Faith Challenge:

Write a prayer for your future and read it each morning this week.

Riddle:

Why did the calendar pray?

Prayer For MY FUTURE

Prayer For MY FUTURE

23. Trusting God's Timing

Scripture: "He makes everything beautiful in its time." – Ecclesiastes 3:11

Waiting stinks, especially when it feels like God's taking forever. But remember, His timing is like cake batter: it's not ready until it's baked through. I know sometimes, it feels like everyone else's life is moving faster than yours, your friends are getting what they prayed for, achieving goals, or hitting milestones while you're… waiting. You might start thinking, "Did God forget about me?" But the truth is, He hasn't.

Trusting God's timing means believing that He knows exactly when you're ready for what you're asking for. It's about remembering that delays aren't denials, they're part of God's perfect plan to prepare you. Just like you wouldn't take cookies out of the oven before they're done,

God won't give you something before it's ready, or before you are.

When you trust His timing, you can rest instead of stress. While you're waiting, He's working, shaping you into the strong, wise, and confident person you're meant to be.

Reflective Questions

What am I waiting for right now? ________________________
____

How can I trust God while I wait? ______________________
____
____

What's one way you can show patience this week? ________
____

Faith Challenge:
Write down three things you're waiting on God for.
Next to each one, write a short prayer like, "God, I trust
Your timing with this."

1. I'm believing and waiting for: ______________________
____
____
Short Prayer: ______________________________________
2. I'm believing and waiting for: ______________________
____
____
Short Prayer: ______________________________________
3. I'm believing and waiting for: ______________________
____
____
Short Prayer: ______________________________________

**Each day this week, thank Him in advance for working
things out, even if you can't see it yet.**

Riddle:
Why did the clock pray for patience?
Why did the clock stay calm during the storm?

 ## 24. Identity in Christ

Your identity isn't defined by looks, grades, friends, or social media, it's defined by who God says you are. You are His beloved, created with a purpose, and equipped with gifts only you have.

When you know your identity in Christ: you don't need everyone's approval, you make choices based on faith, not fear, you walk confidently, knowing your value is unshakable.

2 Corinthians 5:17 says, "Therefore, if anyone is in Christ, the new creation has come: The old has gone, the new is here!" That means your past mistakes, doubts, or insecurities don't define you.

In Christ, you are brand new, valuable, and unstoppable. Knowing who you are in Him helps you glow with confidence, act with purpose, and live a life full of hope and faith.

Scripture: 2 Corinthians 5:17 – "If anyone is in Christ, the new creation has come."

Reflective Questions:

How does being in Christ change how I see myself? ________
____

____

What labels from others do I need to let go of?

____

____

How can I remind myself daily of my identity in Christ?

____

____

Who encourages me to embrace my true self?

____

____

How can I show Christ's love through my actions?

____

____

Faith Challenge:

Write down five things that make you a "new creation" in Christ.

1. ____
2. ____
3. ____
4. ____
5. ____

Riddle:
Why did the butterfly go to church?

 ## 25. Overcoming Doubt

Doubt happens to everyone, even people who love God. You might wonder: "Can I do this?" or "Does God really hear me?" That's normal! The key is not letting doubt control your heart. Mark 9:24 says, "Lord, I believe; help my unbelief."

Overcoming doubt means:

- Turning your worries into prayers
- Reminding yourself of God's promises (like Philippians 4:13, "I can do all things through Christ who strengthens me.")
- Trusting God even when you don't have all the answers
- Surrounding yourself with people who encourage your faith.

Even the strongest faith has "umm… are you sure, God?" moments. Doubt doesn't disqualify you, it invites you to dig deeper, and grow your faith. When you choose to trust God anyway, your confidence and glow grow stronger.

End each day by thanking God for helping you trust Him even when you don't have all the answers, because every time you choose faith over fear, your spiritual muscles grow stronger!

Reflective Questions (Overcoming Doubt):

What's something I've doubted lately?

____

____

How has God proven Himself before?

____

____

What kinds of situations make you start to doubt yourself
or God the most?

____

____

How can you turn your next "What if?" thought into a
prayer instead of a worry?

____

____

Who in your life helps strengthen your faith when you're
feeling uncertain, and how can you be that person for
someone else?

____

____

Faith Challenge:
This week, whenever doubt tries to sneak in, pause and turn
it into a "faith flip." Write down the doubtful thought, then
rewrite it as a faith statement using God's Word. For
example: **Doubt:** "I'm not good enough." **Faith Flip:** "I can
do all things through Christ who strengthens me."
(Philippians 4:13)

Riddle: Why did the cloud stop doubting the rain?

 26. Perseverance

Life can feel like a marathon with hills, puddles, and unexpected detours, that make you want to give up. Perseverance means keeping going even when it's hard, staying focused on your goals, trusting God through every challenge, and not quitting when things get tough.

Perseverance looks like:

- Praying when you're tired or discouraged
- Working hard even when progress feels slow
- Believing setbacks are setup for growth
- Keeping your eyes on God's bigger plan, not just the obstacles.

James 1:12 says, "Blessed is the one who perseveres under trial because, having stood the test, that person will receive the crown of life that the Lord has promised to those who love him." Perseverance strengthens your faith, builds character, and shows the world that your glow **isn't** temporary, it's rooted in God's strength and purpose.

When you persevere, you grow stronger, wiser, and closer to God. Your glow doesn't come from the easy moments, it shines brightest when you keep going despite challenges.

When things get tough, keep running, even if it's more of a faith shuffle. Every step forward counts, even the small ones.

Perseverance means keeping your eyes on God. To persevere is also to continuing to work toward your goals, even when progress is slow. You have to trust that some setbacks are temporary and part of God's plan.

Here are a few funny examples of perseverance:
- "Like when your eyeliner smudges, but you start over again because quitters don't get perfect wings."
- "Perseverance is finishing that 1,000-piece puzzle even though your cat keeps sitting on it."
- "It's trying to keep your cool when your phone autocorrects 'amen' to 'and men.'"
- "Like waiting for your Wi-Fi to reconnect, faith, patience, and just a tiny bit of frustration."
- "When you keep studying even though your brain checked out three snacks ago."

Scripture:

Galatians 6:9 "Let us not become weary in doing good."

Reflective Questions (Perseverance):

Scripture: "Let us run with endurance the race set before us." – Hebrews 12:1
Scripture: Galatians 6:9 – "Let us not become weary in doing good."

When have I felt like giving up?
____

____

How did God help me push through?
____

____

What goals am I committed to finishing?
____

____

Who encourages me to keep going?
____

____

How can I remind myself that perseverance pays off?
____

____

What's something I don't want to give up on?
____

____

Faith Challenge:
Set one small goal this week and finish it with God's help.

Riddle:
Why did the runner bring prayer shoes?
Why did the sneakers praise God?

Teen Tip #5

**Don't Compare, Celebrate Your Journey
Comparison steals joy. Your story is
special and unfolding right on time.**

27. Forgiveness

Forgiveness isn't always easy, but it's one of the most powerful ways to free your heart. Forgiving others (and yourself!) doesn't mean you're okay with what happened, it means you're choosing peace instead of carrying hurt.

Forgiveness looks like:
- Letting go of anger or grudges
- Praying for the person who hurt you
- Remembering God forgives us, so we can forgive others (Matthew 6:14-15)
- Choosing love and kindness even when it's hard

Ephesians 4:32 says, "Be kind and compassionate to one another, forgiving each other, just as in Christ God forgave you."

Forgiveness doesn't just heal relationships, it heals your heart and helps your light shine brighter. When you forgive, you free yourself to live joyfully and confidently.

Forgiving doesn't mean forgetting, it means you make a choice to free your heart, let go of grudges, and watch God heal your soul.

Forgiveness

Scripture: Ephesians 4:32, "Be kind and compassionate to one another, forgiving each other, just as in Christ God forgave you."

Reflective Questions:

Who do I need to forgive?

____

____

How does holding onto anger affect me?

____

____

How can I ask God to help me forgive?

____

____

What feelings do I need to release?

____

____

How can forgiveness bless others and myself?

____

____

Faith Challenge:
Pray for someone who has hurt you and ask God to help you forgive.

Riddle:
Why did the heart open a gift?

# 28. Forgiving "YOURSELF"

Believe it or not, everyone makes mistakes, some big, some small. But holding on to guilt or regret only weighs you down and dims your glow. Forgiving **yourself** doesn't mean ignoring your mistakes; it means learning, growing, and letting God heal your heart.

Forgiving yourself looks like: admitting what went wrong without shame, praying for God's guidance and strength, letting go of self-blame and negative thoughts, choosing to move forward and make better choices.

You can't heal if you keep picking the same scar. God already forgave you, now it's your turn. Let go of guilt and grab grace.1 John 1:9 says, "If we confess our sins, He is faithful and just and will forgive us our sins and purify us from all unrighteousness." That means God already forgives you, now it's your turn to accept it and keep glowing.

Scripture: "There is no *condemnation* for those in Christ Jesus." Romans 8:1

What is condemnation????

Condemnation is that voice that says, "You messed up too bad," or "God can't forgive you this time." But that's not God talking—that's fear and shame lying to you. God's voice speaks love and forgiveness.

Reflective Questions:

What's one mistake you're still being hard on yourself about, and how might God want you to see it differently?
____
____
____

How does holding onto guilt or regret affect your peace and joy? _____________________________________
____
____

What's one thing you've learned or grown from because of a past mistake? _________________________________
____
____

How can you remind yourself each day that God has already forgiven you? ________________________________
____
____

What does it look like for you to "keep glowing" after forgiving yourself? _________________________________
____
____

Faith Challenge:
This week, write a short letter to yourself from God's perspective, full of grace, forgiveness, and love. Read it every day to remind yourself that you are forgiven, loved, and free. Then, each time negative self-talk sneaks in, say out loud: "God forgave me, so I forgive me too."

Riddle:
I'm broken by guilt but mended by grace,
I heal when you stop the endless chase.
You can't buy me or earn me, though you might try—
What am I?

Letters of "Forgiveness"

Dear, ___________________

____

____

____

____

Dear, ___________________

____

____

____

____

Dear, ___________________

____

____

____

____

Dear, ___________________

____

____

____

____

Dear, ___________________

____

____

____

____

Letters of "Forgiveness"

Dear, ________________

Dear, ________________

Dear, ________________

Dear, ________________

Dear, ________________

29. Speaking Life

The words you speak have power, seriously, they do! Speaking life means using your words to uplift, encourage, and bless yourself and others instead of tearing down. Words can hurt, but they can also heal, motivate, and bring hope.

Speaking life looks like:
- Complimenting and encouraging friends (and yourself!)
- Replacing negative self-talk with positive truths
- Speaking truth in love, not gossiping or judging and Praying over your words before you speak

Proverbs 18:21 says, "The tongue has the power of life and death, and those who love it will eat its fruit."

When you choose to speak life, your words build confidence, strengthen relationships, and help your light shine brighter than ever.
Your words can build or break. Speak like your mouth is a microphone for Heaven, kind, true, and full of love.

Riddle:
Why did the words dance?

When was the last time someone's words deeply encouraged you?

____

____

How did that impact your day or mindset?

____

____

What kinds of words do you most often speak to yourself — life-giving or discouraging?

____

____

How can you make your everyday conversations more uplifting and full of grace?

____

____

In what situations do you find it hardest to "speak life," and why?

____

____

How might your relationships change if you made a habit of praying over your words before speaking?

____

____

Faith Challenge:
This week, make a conscious effort to "speak life" every day, encourage at least one person with genuine words, and replace any negative self-talk with a Bible-based truth. End each day by thanking God for the power of your words and asking Him to use them for good.

Riddle:
I'm light as a feather, yet I can crush a heart.
I travel without feet, and my mark can't depart.
What am I?

 30. Patience

Patience isn't just about waiting, it's about trusting God's timing and staying calm while things unfold. Life can feel slow or unfair, but God has a plan, and learning to wait can teach you strength, trust, and self-control.

Patience looks like:

- Taking a deep breath instead of getting frustrated
- Trusting that God's timing is perfect
- Persevering through challenges without giving up
- Praying for guidance while you wait for answers

Patience strengthens your faith, helps you make better choices, and keeps your glow steady even in tough seasons.

Waiting isn't easy, but God is working even when you don't see it. Patience is proof you trust His timing.

Scripture: Psalm 27:14 "Wait for the Lord; be strong and take heart."

Reflective Questions:

What am I waiting for right now? _______________________
____
____

How does waiting test my faith? _______________________
____

Who helps me stay patient? ___________________________
____

How can I use waiting time wisely? ____________________
____

What verse reminds me to trust God's timing? _________
____
____
____

If you don't know a verse, here are a few:

Galatians 6:9 (NIV), "Let us not become weary in doing good, for at the proper time we will reap a harvest if we do not give up." A reminder that good things take time — keep doing the right thing even when it's hard.

Psalm 37:7 (NIV), "Be still before the Lord and wait patiently for him; do not fret when people succeed in their ways, when they carry out their wicked schemes." Waiting on God's timing is not wasting time, it's trusting His plan.

Romans 12:12 (NIV), "Be joyful in hope, patient in affliction, faithful in prayer." Patience is part of a strong faith, keep your hope and prayers steady through tough moments.

Faith Challenge:

Practice waiting without complaining in one situation this week.

Riddle: Why did the clock pray?

31. Helping Others

God didn't just create us to look out for ourselves, He wants us to share love, kindness, and support with the people around us. Helping others isn't just good for them, it also strengthens your heart and your faith.

Helping others looks like:

- Listening and offering encouragement to friends or family
- Volunteering or serving in your community
- Being kind to someone who feels left out
- Using your talents to bless others, big or small

Even small acts of kindness can change someone's world. Smile, listen, or lend a hand, God uses your heart to bless others. Helping others isn't just about big acts, it's in the small stuff too. Smiles, prayers, and kind words change lives more than you know.

Galatians 5:13 says, "Serve one another humbly in love." Every small act of kindness is a way to shine God's light and make the world a better place. When you help others, you grow in empathy, patience, and love, and your own joy and glow multiply.

Scripture: Philippians 2:4, "Look not only to your own interests, but also to the interests of others."

Scripture: "Let us not grow weary in doing good."
Galatians 6:9

Reflective Questions:

How have I helped someone recently?

____

____

Who could I serve this week?

____

____

How does helping others make me feel?

____

____

How can I involve God in my acts of kindness?

____

____

What talents or gifts can I use to bless others?

____

____

Faith Challenge:
Do one intentional act of kindness today.

Riddle:
Why did kindness carry a backpack?

Riddle:
Why did the hands go to church?

 **32. Identity in Christ**

Your identity isn't defined by looks, grades, friends, or social media, it's defined by who God says you are. You are His beloved, created with a purpose, and equipped with gifts only you have.

When you know your identity in Christ:
- You don't need everyone's approval
- You make choices based on faith, not fear
- You walk confidently, knowing your value is unshakable

2 Corinthians 5:17 says, "Therefore, if anyone is in Christ, the new creation has come: The old has gone, the new is here!" That means your past mistakes, doubts, or insecurities don't define you. In Christ, you are brand new, valuable, and unstoppable.
Knowing who you are in Him helps you glow with confidence, act with purpose, and live a life full of hope and faith.

Scripture:
"You are a chosen generation." 1 Peter 2:9

Reflective Questions:

What are some things you've let define you that don't truly reflect who God says you are? _______________________________

____

How does knowing your identity in Christ change the way you see yourself or handle pressure from others? _________

____

What gifts or talents do you think God gave you to make a difference in the world? _______________________________

____

____

When have you felt most confident or at peace knowing you are loved by God? _______________________________

____

How can you remind yourself daily that your worth comes from God, not from what others think? _______________________

____

Faith Challenge:

This week, make a "Who I Am in Christ" list. Write down at least five truths from Scripture about your identity (for example: I am loved, I am chosen, I am forgiven, I am enough, I am God's masterpiece). Post the list somewhere you'll see it often, your mirror, phone lock screen, or journal, and speak those truths over yourself every morning.

Riddle:

I'm not what the world can label or rate,
No likes or follows decide my fate.
Born again, I stand brand new,
What am I when Christ lives in you?

Why did the crown go to church?

33. Dealing with Peer Pressure

Peer pressure is real, friends, social media, or even classmates can make you feel like you have to do something you're not comfortable with. But **here's the truth**: you don't have to follow the crowd.

Dealing with peer pressure means:
- Listening to your values and what God says about right and wrong
- Saying "no" respectfully and confidently when something doesn't feel right
- Surrounding yourself with friends who lift you up, not drag you down
- Remembering that God's approval matters more than anyone else's

Romans 12:2 says, "Do not conform to the pattern of this world, but be transformed by the renewing of your mind." Staying true to your faith and values helps you make choices that honor God and protect your glow.
When you stand firm, you'll not only respect yourself, you'll inspire others to do the same.

It can be easy to say yes when everyone else is doing it, but saying no can take courage. Stand firm, trust God, and be the trendsetter He made you to be.

Reflective Questions:

When have I felt pressured by peers?

____

____

How can I stand firm without being mean?

____

____

Who supports me in making godly choices?

____

____

How does God help me resist temptation?

____

____

What can I do when I feel unsure about a decision?

____

____

Faith Challenge:
Write down one area where you will say "no" this week and pray for courage.

Riddle:
Why did the shoes say no?

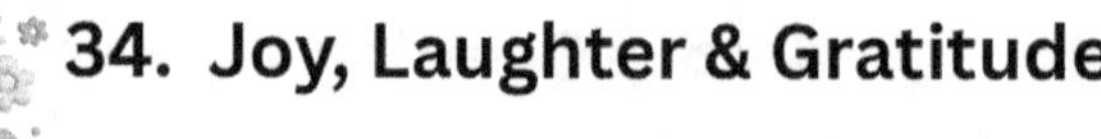

34. Joy, Laughter & Gratitude

Joy is a deep, lasting happiness that comes from trusting God, not just from things going your way. Gratitude is noticing the blessings around you and saying, "Thank You, God!" even in the small stuff. Small blessings can fill your heart when you focus on God. Together, joy and gratitude keep your heart light and your spirit glowing. Understand that joy is contagious, and gratitude is the spark.

Practicing joy and gratitude looks like:
- Thanking God daily for your blessings, big and small
- Celebrating the good in life, even when things are tough
- Focusing on what you have instead of what you don't
- Sharing your joy and positivity with others.

1 Thessalonians 5:18 says, "Give thanks in all circumstances; for this is God's will for you in Christ Jesus."

When you live with joy and gratitude, life feels brighter, your faith grows stronger, and your glow is contagious.

Joy, Laughter & Gratitude

We know that life can get heavy, with school, friends, family, and all the drama. But God wants you to experience joy, even in the middle of the chaos. Joy isn't just happiness that depends on things going your way; it's a deep, lasting sense of peace and gladness that comes from Him.

Laughter is like a superpower, it lifts your mood, strengthens friendships, and reminds you not to take life too seriously. Ecclesiastes 3:4 says there's "a time to weep and a time to laugh." That means God created laughter for a reason!

When you choose joy and laugh through life's challenges: you trust God even when things are hard, you spread positivity to those around you, you keep your heart light and your glow strong.

Remember: Laughing at silly things isn't being childish, it's embracing God's gift of joy. Laughter is like soul sparkle, it makes everything brighter. Even Jesus had a sense of humor (imagine walking on water and pretending to race the disciples!).

Scripture:

Proverbs 17:22, "A cheerful heart is good medicine."

Scripture: Nehemiah 8:10 – "The joy of the Lord is your strength."

Reflective Questions:

What brings me joy today? ____

How can I spread joy to others? ____________________________

What blessings do I often overlook? ____________________________

How does gratitude help me through tough days? __________

Who can I thank this week for encouraging me? __________

Faith Challenge: Write a list of ten things you are thankful for and post it where you can see it every day.

____________________   ____________________

____________________   ____________________

____________________   ____________________

____________________   ____________________

____________________   ____________________

Riddle: Why did the heart sing all week?

Teen Tip #6

Pray First, Worry Less
Prayer brings peace. When you give your worries to God, your heart becomes lighter.

35. Faith-Filled & Fearless

Being faith-filled means trusting God completely, even when things feel scary, uncertain, or overwhelming. Being fearless doesn't mean you won't feel fear, it means you face it with God by your side.

Faith-filled and fearless looks like:
- Praying and trusting God when you're nervous about a test, performance, or new opportunity
- Standing up for what's right, even if it's not the popular choice
- Believing that God's plan is bigger than your fears
- Encouraging others with courage and hope.

Isaiah 41:10 says, "So do not fear, for I am with you; do not be dismayed, for I am your God. I will strengthen you and help you; I will uphold you with my righteous right hand."

When you live faith-filled and fearless, your confidence comes from God, not people or circumstances. You shine boldly, take risks for good, and inspire others to trust God too.
This is your anthem!

Faith-filled and fearless doesn't mean you're never scared, it means you show up anyway, knowing God's got you covered.

Scripture: "Be strong and courageous… for the Lord your God is with you." Joshua 1:9

Reflective Questions:

What does being "fearless in faith" mean to me? _____________

____

____

How has God helped me be brave before? _____________

____

____

____

____

Faith Challenge:

Write a personal affirmation or prayer declaring yourself Faith-Filled & Fearless.

____

____

____

____

____

Riddle:

Why did courage skip the panic party?

YOU DID IT!!!!
End of Journal Reflective Questions

How have I grown in faith through this journal?

____

____

____

Which topics were most meaningful to me and why? _______________________________________

____

How can I continue applying what I've learned?

____

____

Who can I encourage with my faith? _____________

____

____

What prayer or promise will I carry with me moving forward? ________________________________

____

____

Final Riddle: Why did the journal smile at the end? **Because it knew you're unstoppable with God!**

Scripture: Joshua 1:9 "Be strong and courageous. Do not be afraid; do not be discouraged, for the Lord your God will be with you wherever you go."

Dear God,
Thank You for creating me,
loving me, and guiding me.
Help me walk boldly, speak life, and
shine Your light wherever I go.
Teach me to trust Your timing, embrace
my worth, and be Faith-Filled &
Fearless every day. Amen.

Affirmation: "I am loved.
I am strong.
I am Faith-Filled & Fearless."

Riddle Answers

1.👉 Your God-given worth.
2.👉 Because it didn't want to be taken out of context.
3.👉 Because it wanted God to lead the point!
4.👉 Because it wanted to reflect God's glory!
5.👉 It needed to rest in God's timing!
6.👉 Because hate got tired halfway through!
7.👉 To stick with you through everything!
8.👉 It didn't want to lose connection with God!
9.👉 It was ready for a shower of blessings!
10.👉 To get filled with the Living Water!
11.👉 It refused to let go of the past!
12.👉 Because it saw a masterpiece!
13.👉 To get better reception with God!
14.👉 Because it was plugged into its power source!
15.👉 It wanted to make smart decisions!
16.👉 To have a taste of togetherness!
17.👉 So it wouldn't pop off!
18.👉 It knew God was opening another one!
19.👉 It remembered its own race!

20.👉 It couldn't stop counting blessings!
21.👉 To keep its vision pure!
22.👉 It wanted all its days to be blessed!
23.👉 It was tired of ticking too soon!
👉 Because it trusted that time was on its side!
24.👉 It wanted to remember it's a new creation!
25.👉 Because it finally trusted its own drops!
26.👉 To keep running in faith!
👉 Because they were walking by faith!
27.👉 Because it forgave and received peace!
28.👉 Forgiveness — especially self-forgiveness.
29.👉 Because the Spirit moved them!
👉 The answer is "Words."
30.👉 Because it wanted to tick in God's perfect timing!
31.👉 Because it wanted to carry extra compassion to share!
👉 To lend a helping hand!
32.👉 Your identity in Christ — a new creation!)
👉 Because it wanted to meet the King of Kings!
33.👉 Because they didn't want to follow the wrong path!
34. 👉 Because it counted its blessings!
35. 👉 Because it was too busy trusting God!

Keep Praying. Keep Glowing. Keep Growing.

You made it to the end, great job!

Remember, growing in faith doesn't mean being perfect. It means trusting that God is working in you every day. Keep praying when life feels hard. Keep glowing with kindness and confidence.

Keep growing into the young woman God created you to be.
You are loved. You are chosen. And God isn't finished with your story yet.

"He who began a good work in you will carry it on to completion."
Philippians 1:6